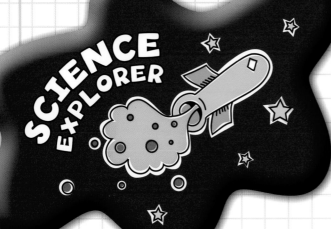

DIGESTION

SUPER COOL
SCIENCE
EXPERIMENTS:
DIGESTION

by Tamra B. Orr

CHERRY LAKE PUBLISHING • ANN ARBOR, MICHIGAN

CHERRY
LAKE
Publishing

A NOTE TO PARENTS AND TEACHERS: Please review the instructions for these experiments before your children do them. Be sure to help them with any experiments you do not think they can safely conduct on their own.

A NOTE TO KIDS: Be sure to ask an adult for help with these experiments when you need it. Always put your safety first!

Published in the United States of America by
Cherry Lake Publishing
Ann Arbor, Michigan
www.cherrylakepublishing.com

Content Editor: Robert Wolffe, EdD,
Professor of Teacher Education,
Bradley University, Peoria, Illinois

Book design and illustration: The Design Lab

Photo Credits: Cover and page 1, ©Soupstock/Dreamstime.com; page
5, ©iStockphoto.com/Soubrette; page 8, ©Noam Armonn, used under
license from Shutterstock, Inc.; page 12, ©PHOTOTAKE Inc./Alamy;
page 16, ©Eraxion/Dreamstime.com; page 20, ©MedicalRF.com/Alamy;
page 25, ©Danilo Ascione, used under license from Shutterstock, Inc.

Library of Congress Cataloging-in-Publication Data
Orr, Tamra.
  Super cool science experiments: Digestion / by Tamra Orr.
     p. cm.—(Science explorer)
  Includes bibliographical references and index.
  ISBN-13: 978-1-60279-518-1   ISBN-10: 1-60279-518-5 (lib. bdg.)
  ISBN-13: 978-1-60279-597-6   ISBN-10: 1-60279-597-5 (pbk.)
  1. Digestion—Juvenile literature. 2. Gastrointestinal system—
Physiology—Juvenile literature. I. Title. II. Title: Digestion. III. Series.
  QP145.O77 2010
  612.3—dc22   2009004775

Cherry Lake Publishing would like to acknowledge the work
of The Partnership for 21st Century Skills. Please visit
www.21stcenturyskills.org for more information.

DIGESTION

TABLE OF CONTENTS

Notes:

Day 1:

Day 2:

Chew on This!

Crunch, crunch, crunch! What comes to mind when you eat a cold, crisp apple? You probably just think it tastes good. But have you ever really thought about how that apple makes its way through your body? Or how you get energy from food? Science is at work inside your body every time you take a bite of food or sip a drink.

If you like to carefully find answers to interesting questions, you are on your way to becoming a scientist. Believe it or not, you can do experiments with things you already have at home. In this book, we'll learn how scientists think. We'll do that by experimenting with the process of digestion. Here's the best part: you'll learn lots of things and have fun at the same time!

Take a bite and start learning about digestion! →

4

First Things First

Models can help you learn more about the digestive system and other parts of the body.

Scientists learn by studying things and people very carefully. Scientists who study humans watch how they develop. They research which parts of the body do different jobs. They figure out how these body parts are connected. They study how important food is for human health and how the digestive system works. Scientists do experiments to see how the body gets and uses nutrients to keep itself healthy.

Good scientists take notes on everything they discover. They write down their observations. Sometimes those observations lead scientists to ask new questions. With new questions in mind, they design experiments to find answers.

When scientists design experiments, they must think very clearly. The way they think about problems is often called the scientific method. What is the scientific method? It's a step-by-step way of finding answers to specific questions. The steps don't always follow the same pattern. Sometimes scientists change their minds. The process often works something like this:

- **Step One:** A scientist gathers the facts and makes observations about one particular thing.
- **Step Two:** The scientist comes up with a question that is not answered by all the observations and facts.
- **Step Three:** The scientist creates a hypothesis. This is a statement of what the scientist thinks is probably the answer to the question.
- **Step Four:** The scientist tests the hypothesis. He or she designs an experiment to see whether the hypothesis is correct. The scientist does the experiment and writes down what happens.

- **Step Five:** The scientist draws a conclusion based on how the experiment turned out. The conclusion might be that the hypothesis is correct. Sometimes, though, the hypothesis is not correct. In that case, the scientist might develop a new hypothesis and another experiment.

In the following experiments, we'll see the scientific method in action. We'll gather some facts and observations about the digestive system. And for each experiment, we'll develop a question and a hypothesis. Next, we'll do an actual experiment to see if our hypothesis is correct. By the end of the experiment, we should know something new about digestion. Scientists, are you ready? Then let's get started!

You'll need a notebook and pen or pencil.

Experiment #1
Open Wide!

Let's find out what happens after you take a bite.

Do you like to eat? We need both food and water to stay alive. The nutrients we get from food give us energy, help us grow, and keep us healthy. You can go about three days at the most without water, before running into some serious problems.

The way your body uses the nutrients in food and drink is called digestion. Can you guess where your digestive system starts? Your mouth! Your mouth, teeth, tongue, and saliva are the first stops on what is actually a very long journey. That journey ends when whatever you take in through your mouth leaves the digestive system.

Your teeth help you by cutting up the big pieces of food so that they fit in your mouth. Your teeth grind and chew those pieces of food so that they are easier and safer to swallow. This grinding action is an important step in the beginning of the process of digestion.

Your tongue plays an important part, too. If you aren't sure what it does, try this: Put a piece of soft bread in the middle of your tongue. While holding the tip of your tongue with your fingers, try to swallow. What happened? Not much! Your tongue's job is to push food to the back of your mouth. If your tongue can't do that, it is almost impossible to swallow.

Have you ever wondered what saliva is really for? It has many jobs. When you put food in your mouth, your saliva begins to break down the chemicals in the food. Until that process happens, your taste buds cannot taste much flavor at all. Does this mean that without saliva your food tastes boring? With that question in mind, come up with a hypothesis. Here is one possibility: **Food does not have much flavor if saliva does not mix with it in our mouth.**

Here's what you'll need:
- A roll of paper towels
- 2 different dry foods, such as crackers and pretzels
- Drinking water

You can snack and experiment at the same time! ↓

Instructions:
1. Use a clean, dry paper towel to dry off your tongue.
2. Take a bite of 1 kind of food. How does it taste? Pay close attention.
3. Take a sip of water to clean out your mouth. Dry off your tongue with another paper towel.
4. Take a bite of the second kind of food. How does it taste?
5. Take another sip of water, but this time, don't dry your tongue.

6. Take a bite of the first type of food you tasted. How does it taste now? Take a sip of water, but don't dry your tongue.

7. Take a bite of the second type of food you tasted. Does it taste different?

Don't forget to write down your observations.

Conclusion:

How does saliva affect the way each food tastes? Based on your observations, you have probably concluded that saliva helps us taste food.

Experiment #2
Down It Goes

esophagus

Your esophaqus is long and skinny.

Where does food go after being chewed? You might think it goes to your stomach, but you would be missing a step. First, it has to go down your esophagus.

The esophagus is a muscular passageway. It is a long, 10-inch (25.4 centimeter) tube that is able to stretch. It connects the back of your throat to your stomach.

When food enters the esophagus, it does not just drop straight down to the stomach. Instead, it is pushed down by strong muscles.

When the food finally reaches the stomach, that organ is ready and waiting! One way the stomach has prepared for the arrival is by creating stomach acid. This is a mixture that helps break down food. The broken-down food will eventually pass along through other parts of the digestive system. There, nutrients will be absorbed and sent where they need to go.

As long as stomach acid stays in the stomach, you shouldn't have problems. A valve there makes sure this happens. But if a person eats too much and overfills the stomach, the food and acid can push up on that valve. The valve may not be able to close properly. What happens then? Think about stomach acid. Do you think substances in the stomach—such as that acid—can go back up into the esophagus? That's a good focus for our next hypothesis. Here is one you might want to test by building a model: **Under certain conditions, food and acid from the stomach can flow up into the esophagus.**

Here's what you'll need:

- 1 large straw
- 1 balloon
- Water

You don't need fancy materials to make models!

Instructions:

1. Push one end of the straw into the balloon opening. Hold the balloon and straw together with your fingers. Your fingers are playing the same role as the valve between your stomach and esophagus. Think of this valve as a ring of muscle. It opens to let food and liquids in. It also prevents food from going back up the esophagus when it closes. If everything is working properly, the food should go on a one-way trip! Be sure to hold the balloon sideways, or horizontally. That is how the stomach sits inside you.

2. Carefully pour water into the balloon through the straw until the balloon is overly full.

3. Lightly squeeze the balloon. What happens?

Conclusion:

In this experiment, the balloon represents your stomach. The straw is your esophagus. The water is the contents of your stomach. What effect does squeezing the balloon have on the water? Squeezing the balloon creates pressure. This extra pressure on the valve (your fingers) pushes the water back up into the straw. This means that stomach acid can go up into the esophagus. When it does, the result is often known as heartburn. Does heartburn have anything to do with your heart? Nope—but the acid does burn your esophagus!

This is amazing!

How long is your digestive system? Here is one way to figure it out. Cut a piece of yarn 10 inches (25.4 cm) long for your esophagus, 8 inches (20.3 cm) long for your stomach, 23 feet (7 m) long for your small intestine, and 59 inches (149.9 cm) long for your large intestine.

Now tape all the pieces of yarn together, end to end. You will find that from beginning to end, an adult's digestive system is about 30 feet (9.1 m) long!

Experiment #3

A Strong Mixer

The stomach has an important job to do.

Your stomach is one of the most important parts of the digestive system. It has several jobs. Much of the stomach wall is made up of sets of powerful muscles. Why does the stomach need these muscles? Are they an important part of breaking down food? Think about it. Come up with a hypothesis, or test this one: **Muscles in the stomach wall help break down food.**

Here's what you'll need:

- ½ cup of vinegar
- 2 resealable plastic bags
- Dry crackers
- Water

Gather your supplies.

Instructions:

1. Pour ¼ cup of vinegar into each plastic bag. Be careful not to spill the vinegar or get any in your eyes. Seal the bags.
2. Take 2 crackers and smash them.
3. Add a tiny bit of water and roll the cracker bits into a ball.
4. Do the same thing with 2 more crackers.

5. Place 1 cracker ball in each bag. Reseal the bags. Set 1 bag aside.
6. Take the other bag in your hands, and slowly and carefully squeeze and release. Use these movements to mash, mix, and break down the cracker ball. What do you see happening? How does the food look?

Squeeze carefully if you don't want a gooey mess to clean up!

Conclusion:

The plastic bags represent your stomach. The vinegar is your stomach acid. The crackers represent chewed-up food. In a very simplified way, squeezing the bag represents the motions of the stomach muscles as they mix the food. How did the food begin to change as you squeezed the bag? Does the food in the squeezed bag look different from the food in the bag that you set to the side? Was your hypothesis correct?

Like a giant mixer, the stomach's strong muscles and powerful acid combine to break down everything it is sent from a solid into a liquid. The amount of time needed for the process to take place or for food to pass through the stomach varies. The type of food eaten is one factor that can make a difference. The process can take about 2.5 to 5 hours. When the stomach is finished, it sends the mixture to the next stop in the process: the small intestine. This mixture is called chyme.

Your stomach is important, but did you know that it is actually possible to live without one? The stomach is helpful because it holds on to our food. But the small intestine is where most of the digestion that breaks food down to usable nutrients takes place. The stomach allows us to eat less often than we might have to if food went directly to the small intestine. Without a stomach, you would also probably have to eat smaller meals. But your body would adapt to life without a stomach.

Experiment #4

A Digestive Powerhouse

small intestine

Wave-like muscle movements push food through your small intestine.

The small intestine is really the star of the digestive system. It is about 2 inches (5.1 cm) around and is packed tightly inside you, right under your stomach. It is the longest part of the digestive tract. If you were able to stretch out an adult's small intestine from end to end, it would be about 23 feet (7 m) long. Inside the small intestine is where almost all of the actual digestion takes place. The chyme that comes from your stomach won't do you any good until your small intestine comes into play. It begins to break down and absorb the vitamins, minerals, proteins, complex carbohydrates, and fats in the chyme.

No star can perform without a few helpers, right? The same is true of the small intestine. The co-stars that help it do its job are the pancreas, liver, and gallbladder. The pancreas makes special juices that help the body digest fats, starches, and proteins. The liver makes a product called bile, which also helps with fat digestion. What is the gallbladder's job? It acts as a warehouse that stores the bile the liver makes. It sends it out whenever the body needs it.

Think of your small intestine as a very long toothpaste tube. Just as you squeeze the tube with your fingers, the intestine squeezes food from one end to the other. The walls of the intestine are covered with tiny projections called villi. Nutrients pass through the surface of the small intestine and travel to the rest of your body. The villi increase the surface area of the small intestine to help more nutrients pass through it into your blood. Do you think the size of something affects whether or not it can pass through the wall of the small intestine? That question is the basis of our next hypothesis: **If something is too big, it can't pass through the wall of the small intestine.** Let's test this hypothesis using a model to represent the small intestine.

Here's what you'll need:
- 2 Styrofoam cups of the same size
- Water
- 1 tablespoon of black pepper
- 2 tablespoons of sugar
- 1 paper towel

You may already have these items in your kitchen.

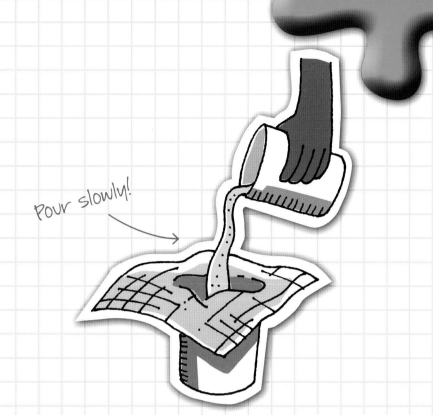

Pour slowly!

Instructions:

1. Fill 1 cup halfway with water.
2. Add the black pepper and sugar to the water and mix well.
3. Place the paper towel over the second cup. Push the paper towel down into the cup about a third of the way down. The rest of the paper towel should hang over the sides of the cup.
4. Slowly pour the water solution through the paper towel into the second cup. Look at what is left on the paper towel. What passed through it and what didn't? You probably can see that the coarse pieces of black pepper were blocked by the paper towel.
5. Take a sip of the water that filtered into the second cup. Does it taste sweet?

Conclusion:
The paper towel represents the wall of the small intestine and its villi. The bits of pepper represent larger solids in the small intestine. How does this help you understand what passes through the villi? Once the nutrients have passed through the villi, they go into the bloodstream and throughout your body. The water in the second cup represents what passes into your bloodstream. The water tasted sweet because the sugar dissolved and became small enough to pass through the villi. The sugar is kind of like the nutrients that have been broken down enough to be absorbed by the body. Was your hypothesis correct?

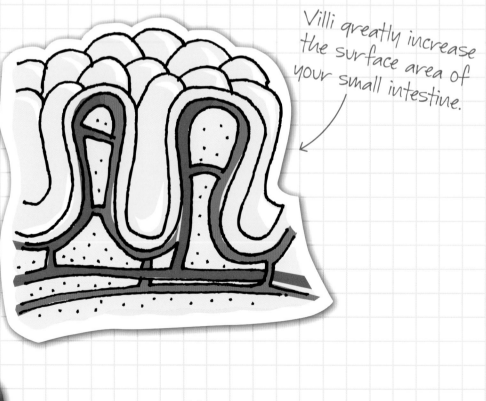

Villi greatly increase the surface area of your small intestine.

Experiment #5
The End of the Journey

The large intestine looks white in this X-ray.

Hours and hours ago, you had something to eat and the digestive process began. Now that food has traveled through your esophagus, stomach, and small intestine. All that is left of it is the waste that your body does not need. That is where the large intestine's job kicks in. Our long journey is almost over.

The large intestine is actually much shorter than the small intestine. It is larger around—usually 3 to 4 inches (7.6 to 10.2 cm)—but only 5 feet (1.5 m) long. One section of the intestine is called the colon. It is here that the body has its last chance to absorb water from the digested food material. This is also where millions of hungry bacteria break down the unused bits of what is left.

Has your family ever baked bread? An organism called yeast is used to make bread. When the yeast feeds, it produces gas. This gas helps bread dough to rise. Do you think that the bacteria in the large intestine also make gas when they break down food? Let's find out. Come up with a hypothesis, or test this one: **Bacteria in the large intestine produce gas when they break down food.**

Here's what you'll need:
- 1 banana
- A blender
- A glass flask or other glass container with a narrow neck
- 1 medium-sized balloon

No blender? Maybe you can borrow one from a friend.

26

Observe the flask at the same time each day.

Instructions:

1. Blend the banana in a blender until it is smooth. Be very careful when using a blender. Ask an adult for help if you need it.
2. Place the mixture into the flask. The flask represents your large intestine. The banana goo represents food matter.
3. Attach the balloon to the mouth of the flask.
4. Choose a safe place to keep your flask where it will not be disturbed. Try to find a warm spot if possible.
5. Every day for 5 days, spend a few minutes looking at the mush in the flask. Write down what you see and how it changes. Does the balloon look different?

Conclusion:

What happens to the banana goo? What happens to the balloon? What does the balloon fill up with? If you said "gas," you're right. If you let it out, it would be like one huge . . . you know what! Bacteria in the large intestine release gas when they break down food. This gas adds up inside your large intestine. Can you guess what happens to it? Eventually, you release it—otherwise known as passing gas.

From the large intestine, waste products are pushed into the very last part of the digestive process: the rectum. This is also where the gas comes out! From there, the waste leaves your body and is flushed away. The trip that started many hours ago has finally ended. The nutrients in the food you ate have spread throughout your body, helping you grow and stay healthy.

Have you ever noticed that corn kernels tend to leave your body looking exactly like they did on the way in? Corn kernels are very difficult to break down. We also tend not to chew each piece of corn as well as we could. This often means that a number of kernels slip through the entire digestive system virtually untouched!

Experiment #6

Do It Yourself!

Well, scientists? Where do you go from here? Pick one area of digestion that interests you, and develop a hypothesis and experiment. Be creative. For example, create another experiment that has to do with the esophagus. Do you think you must always be sitting in an upright position in order for the esophagus to send liquids or food to the stomach? Come up with a hypothesis. Then you could try carefully swallowing a small sip of water or bite of food while in different positions: standing, sitting, and lying on your side. Be very careful not to choke. Run your experiment, and record the results.

Digestion is interesting, isn't it? Food goes through many twists and turns before leaving your body. Remember that long journey the next time you grab a bite!

GLOSSARY

bile (BILE) a liquid made by the liver that helps digest fats

chyme (KYME) the partly liquid form of food produced in the stomach while being digested

conclusion (kuhn-KLOO-zhuhn) a final decision, thought, or opinion

digestion (dye-JESS-chuhn) the process in which the stomach and other organs change food into forms that can be absorbed by the body

hypothesis (hy-POTH-uh-sihss) a logical guess about what will happen in an experiment

method (METH-uhd) a way of doing something

nutrients (NOO-tree-uhntss) things that are needed by plants, animals, and humans to stay healthy

observations (ob-zur-VAY-shuhnz) things that are seen or noticed with one's senses

rectum (REK-tuhm) the lowest section of the large intestine, ending at the anus

saliva (suh-LYE-vuh) the fluid in the mouth that helps a person swallow and start to digest food

villi (VIL-eye) fingerlike structures on the walls of the intestines that help absorb nutrients

FOR MORE INFORMATION

BOOKS

Burstein, John. *The Dynamic Digestive System: How Does My Stomach Work?* New York: Crabtree Publishing Company, 2009.

Green, Jen. *Digestion.* North Mankato, MN: Stargazer Books, 2006.

Petrie, Kristin. *The Digestive System.* Edina, MN: ABDO Publishing Company, 2007.

WEB SITES

Discovery Kids—Your Digestive System

yucky.discovery.com/flash/body/pg000126.html
Find fun facts about digestion

KidsHealth—Your Digestive System

kidshealth.org/kid/htbw/digestive_system.html
A great resource for information on how the digestive system works

PBS Kids—ZOOMsci: Tongue Map

pbskids.org/zoom/activities/sci/tonguemap.html
Try this fun activity and learn about how your tongue tastes different flavors

INDEX

About the → Author

Tamra Orr is the author of more than 200 nonfiction books for readers of all ages. She loves doing research—especially if eating something tasty is part of the process. Orr lives in the Pacific Northwest with her husband, three teenagers, a cat, and a dog. She has a teaching degree from Ball State University and in her few minutes of spare time, she likes to write letters, read books, and look at the snowcapped mountains.